My Christmas
Art Class

Nellie Shepherd

A Dorling Kindersley Book

DK

LONDON, NEW YORK, MUNICH, MELBOURNE, AND DELHI

Editor Penny Smith
Senior Designer Wendy Bartlet
Designer Victoria Long
Additional Design Melanie Leighton
Production Shivani Pandey
Photography Stephen Hepworth

For my brother Stephen Hepworth (A Wonderful Photographer!)

ACKNOWLEDGMENTS
With thanks to: Jean Gollner, Anne Lumb, David Hansel (Memery Crystal),
Joseph Whitworth Centre, Broomhall Nursery School and Early Years
Centre, and all the children who took part in the photography.
Special thanks to the artists: Peggy Atherton, Emma Hardy,
Jane McDonald, Katie Noorlander, and Allie Scott.

First published in Great Britain in 2004
by Dorling Kindersley Limited
80 Strand, London WC2R ORL
A Penguin Company
2 4 6 8 10 9 7 5 3 1

See
Dorling Kindersley's
complete catalogue at
www.dk.com

A CIP catalogue record for this book
is available from the British Library

ISBN: 1-4053-0569-X

Colour reproduction by GRB Editrice, Italy
Printed and bound in China by Toppan

Where to find things

My Christmas Art Class

Here's a book filled with funky, festive things to make at Christmas time.

Yippee, it's Christmas – my favourite time of year! I'd love everyone to have a happy Christmas making things to play with and give away.
In this book you'll find fantastic festive skittles, a reindeer headdress, gift wrapping ideas, a mega pop-up Christmas card, and lots more.
Get out your glue and your glitter and go for it!

Love
Nellie x

Read Nellie's Christmas tips on page 46.

Basic kit

As well as the equipment pictured with each project, you will need the following basic kit:

card	glitter
paper	glitter glue
tissue paper	wool
PVA glue	pom–poms
tape	wiggly eyes
paintbrushes	felt
scissors	
felt–tip pens	
stapler	

Keep your art kit in a box so you can find it easily!

Helping hand

All the projects in this book are designed for young children to make, but they should only be attempted under adult supervision. Extra care should be taken when using sharp equipment, such as scissors, staplers, and pipe cleaners, and with small objects that may cause choking. Only use PVA or other non–toxic, water–soluble glue.

Snowman Sam

woolly hat

Here's a little
Snowman
Made from
A pillowcase.
Using bits
Of coloured felt,
Stick a smile
Onto his face.

pillowcase

scarf

You can use...

scarf

pillowcases

pillow

felt

woolly hat

Tot Tip! There's no need to get glue on your best pillow! Simply put it inside a couple of old pillowcases and decorate the top one.

How to make it!

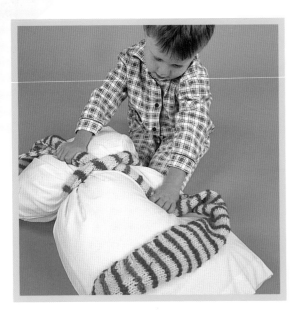

tie

Put your pillowcases on your pillow. Tie a scarf round the pillow to make Snowman Sam's head and body.

cut out

Cut out Sam's felt face – big eyes, pink cheeks, a carrot-shaped nose, and lots of circles for his lovely smiley mouth.

glue

Put a woolly hat on Sam's head, then glue on his felt face.

I'm soft as snow!

stick

Cut out Sam's felt lapels, buttons, pocket, and holly, and stick them on his body. Now he's ready to cuddle!

9

Have a Heart

This lovely heart
Is made from beans.
It can be big or small.
It's the perfect decoration
For your tree or for your wall.

dried kidney beans

Paint

ribbon

You can use...

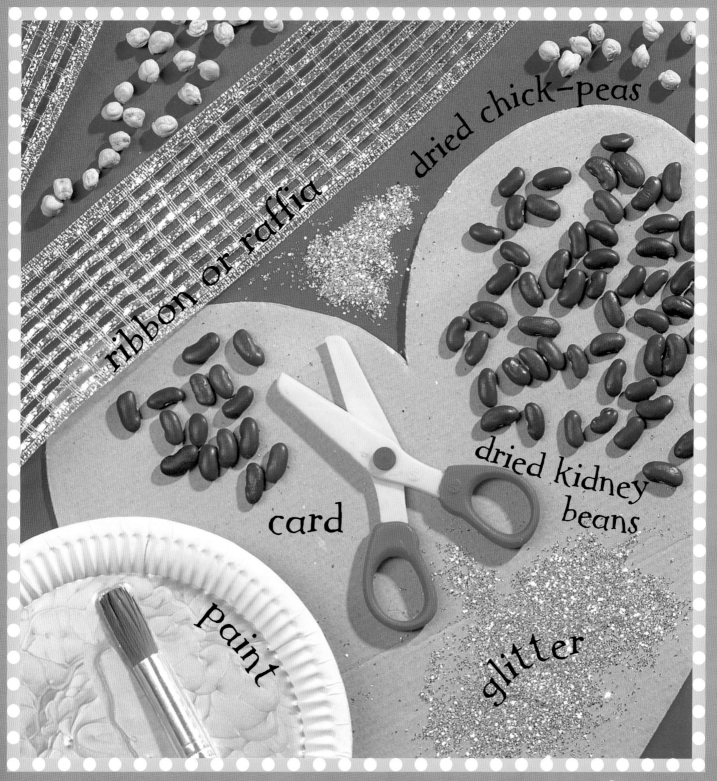

ribbon or raffia

dried chick-peas

dried kidney beans

card

paint

glitter

Tot Tip! Make little hearts to hang on your Christmas tree. You can use dried beans or chick-peas to decorate them.

You can do it!

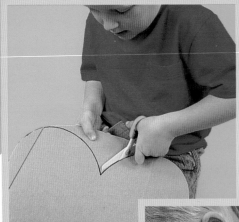

cut out

I love this decoration – it's so incredibly easy to make! Start by drawing a big heart shape on a sturdy piece of card. Then cut it out.

brush

The next thing to do is to brush a thick layer of lovely sticky glue all over your card heart.

place

Place dried beans or chick-peas in the glue, as close together as you can. If you'd like to make a pattern, circles and swirls work brilliantly!

paint

Mix a little glue into your paint. Then paint your heart and sprinkle it with glitter. Glue on a ribbon or raffia bow. Remember to lay your heart flat until it is completely dry.

Kid's talk
"I've got a heart
and it lives in
my tummy."
Georgie, age 4 ¾

Twinkle Star

You're .
Dressed as
A sparkling star,
Shining brightly
From afar.
And as you twinkle,
All will see
Just how star-like
You can be.

ribbon

card

You can use...

card

tissue paper

glue

kitchen foil

ribbon

glitter

shiny jewels

cellophane

shiny paper

stickers

15

Tot Tip!

Would you like a wand to go with your outfit? Then cut out a card star, cover it with glitter, and tape it to the top of a pencil.

Here we go!

big star

Draw and cut out a big card star. Decorate it with kitchen foil, cellophane, or other shiny paper. For extra sparkle, stick on shiny jewels, stickers, or glitter. Staple ribbon to your star so you can hang it round your neck.

star hat

For a lovely star hat, cut a strip of card to fit round your head. Decorate it with tissue paper and glitter. Then staple it together at the back.

staple on a star

Add a fabulous shooting star to your hat. To make one, staple a glittery star to a strip of card, then staple the card to your hat.

twinkle toes

To brighten up your feet, decorate more card stars with glitter and shiny jewels. Thread ribbon through holes in the stars, then tie the stars to your ankles.

Kid's talk
"Twinkle, twinkle,
little star.
How I wonder
what you are."
Mia, age 3

Rosie Reindeer

My name
Is Rosie Reindeer,
And I pull Santa's sleigh.
I help deliver presents
In time for Christmas day!

twig

glitter

18

You can use...

twigs

twigs

glitter

tissue paper

card

card

staples

Tot Tip!

Here's the basic shape you need for your reindeer headdress. Copy it onto a big piece of card.

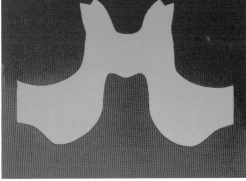

How to make it!

cut out

Cut out your reindeer headdress. Make sure it fits comfortably round your head.

sprinkle

To make beautiful antlers, brush glue over a couple of twigs and sprinkle them with glitter.

decorate

Decorate your card headdress with little balls of scrunched-up tissue paper, sparkly glitter, paper, or felt.

tape

Tape your antlers to your headdress. To make the antlers extra secure, tape squares of card over the ends of the twigs.

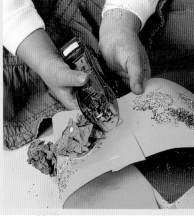

staple

Staple your headdress together at the back. Now you can pretend to be Rosie!

Kid's talk

"Reindeers like Christmas pudding." Amy, age 4

21

Christmas Time!

pipe cleaner

card star

Here's a
Christmas present.
Doesn't it look fine?
Move its hands
Around its face,
And learn
To tell the time.

tick
tock!

tick
tock!

You can use...

box

glitter glue

pipe cleaners

paper fastener

card

tissue paper

glitter

shiny things

stickers

Tot Tip! You can buy number stickers from newsagents, toy shops, and craft shops. Or simply write numbers on your clock using felt-tip pens or glitter glue.

23

Here we go!

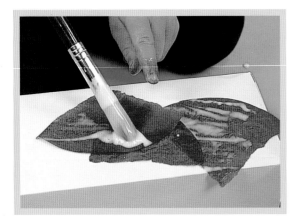

cover

Start making your clock by covering a box with tissue paper. You don't need to be neat – overlapping tissue paper gives a lovely texture.

stick

To make your clock's face, you can stick number stickers on the front of your covered box.

attach

Make two clock hands from card. Glue glitter all over them, then attach them to your clock using a paper fastener.

decorate

Decorate your clock with your own gorgeous design of shiny things and glitter glue.

finish

To finish, staple shiny or glittery card stars to pipe cleaners, and push them into the top of your clock.

24

Kid's talk
"Clocks are
clever because
they know when
it's bedtime."
Joe, age 3 ½

Santa's Skittles

Here's a group of skittles
Standing straight and tall.
Roll your ball towards them.
Which one's going to fall?

pipe cleaner

I'm a pushover!

cotton wool

You can use...

plastic bottles

tissue paper

cotton wool

wool

Ping-Pong balls

glitter glue

shiny things

Paint

crepe paper

fur

pipe cleaners

stickers

You can do it!

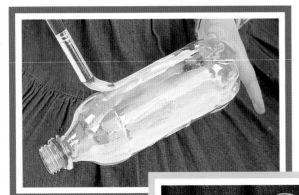

brush

You can copy our skittles or design your own. Make one skittle at a time. Start by brushing glue over a plastic bottle.

wrap

I'm knocked out!

Wrap crepe paper or cotton wool round your sticky bottle.

stick

Stick on pipe-cleaner wings or antlers, shiny buttons, fur trim, and other decorations made from glitter glue, stickers, tissue paper, or anything you fancy.

make a head

Make a head for a character skittle by cutting a hole in a Ping-Pong ball. Push the ball onto your bottle and paint it.

stick again

Stick or draw on your skittle's face. You can make hair from wool, antlers or a headdress from pipe cleaners, hats from card, or use whatever is to hand.

Glitter Birds

Peg these
Little birds
To the branches
Of your tree.
They'll sit there
All through
Christmas
Sparkling merrily.

tissue
paper

I love to
sparkle!

feather

glitter

You can use...

feathers

wiggly eye

lace

tissue paper

peg

card

felt

glitter

Tot Tip! Each glitter bird has a peg taped to the back of it. You can also tape pegs to glittery shapes such as stars or hearts, and peg these to your tree.

Here we go!

draw

Start making a lovely little glitter bird by drawing round a cup on card. Then cut out the circle.

sprinkle

Brush the card circle with glue and sprinkle on lots of glitter. Shake off any excess.

stick

Now stick on a tissue-paper beak and a wiggly eye. Make your bird's wing from card, lace, or felt, and its tail from card or a feather.

tape

Tape a peg to the back of your glitter bird. Then peg the bird on your Christmas tree.

"Real birds
are fluffy,
not glittery."
Samuel, age 5

35

Mega Pop-up Card

pipe cleaner

pop-up fold

fur

tissue paper

This giant Christmas card
Has surprises inside.
Pictures pop up
When you open it wide!

You can use...

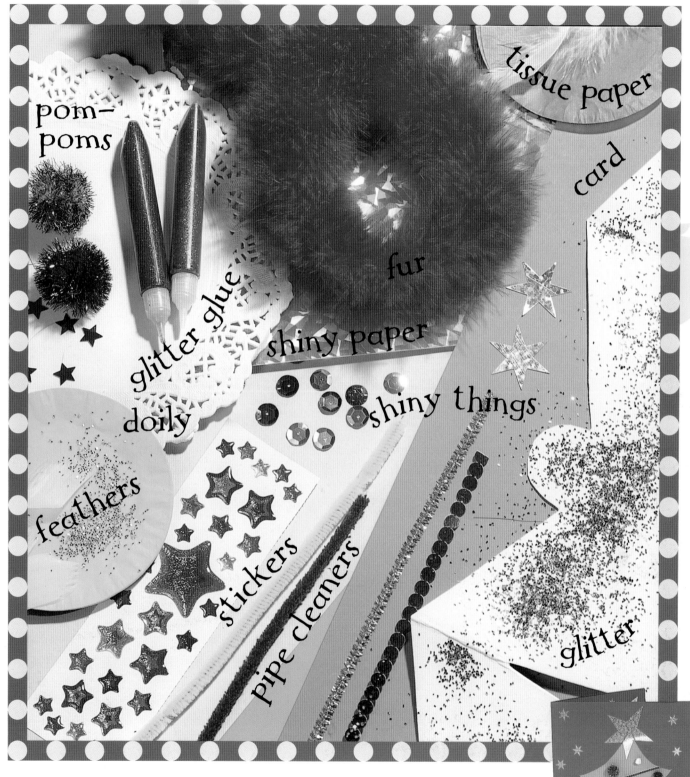

- pom-poms
- tissue paper
- card
- glitter glue
- fur
- shiny paper
- doily
- shiny things
- feathers
- stickers
- pipe cleaners
- glitter

Tot Tip! Don't forget to decorate the front of your card! Simple paper shapes, pom-poms, and shiny things are fun to use and look great!

35

How to make it!

fold

Start making the pop-up part of your Christmas card by folding a big rectangle of card into a "W" shape as shown in this picture.

draw

Draw a Christmas tree on the folded card. Cut out your drawing so you have four trees attached to each other.

glue

Fold an even bigger piece of card in half. Glue the end Christmas trees inside this card, so the two middle trees can pop up. Decorate with glitter, stickers, shiny things, and tissue paper.

more pop-ups

You can make hearts or angels in the same way as your trees. Give the angels faces, dresses, arms, and legs using wool, pipe cleaners, and other bits and bobs.

Mr Santa

cotton wool

balloon

This Mr Santa
Is easy to make.
His tummy is round.
I think he likes cake!

You can use...

felt

wiggly eyes

paper plate

cotton wool

card

balloon

sticky-back paper

Tot Tip! Don't be tempted to remove sticky-back paper or tape once you've stuck them to Mr Santa's balloon body. If you pull them off, he will burst!

You can do it!

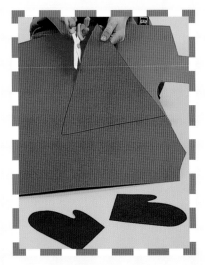

cut out

Cut out all the pieces you need for Mr Santa – card arms, legs, hands, and feet, and a card or felt hat. Blow up his balloon body.

fold

Fold Mr Santa's arms and legs and attach them to his hands and feet. Tape his arms and legs to his balloon body. Dress up Mr Santa – stick on tissue paper, cotton wool, glitter glue, or sticky-back paper.

tape

For Mr Santa's head, tape a paper plate to the knot on his balloon body.

glue

Tape Mr Santa's hat to the paper plate. Then glue on his wiggly eyes, card mouth, and a nose made from card or a pom-pom. Finally, stick on his cotton-wool beard and hair.

Kid's talk
"Mr Santa's big, but not as big as my daddy."
Helena, age 5

It's a Wrap!

Dress up your Christmas parcels
With paper and gift tags, too.
Put them under the Christmas tree
Then see if there's one for you!

fur

card

You can use...

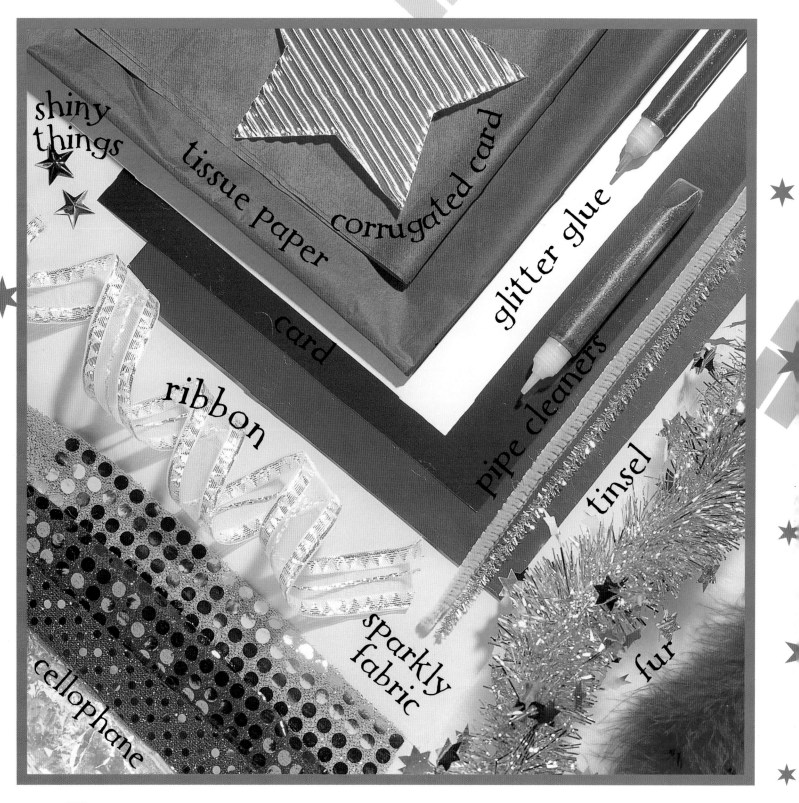

shiny things

tissue paper

corrugated card

glitter glue

card

ribbon

pipe cleaners

tinsel

fur

sparkly fabric

cellophane

Tot Tip! Look around the shops for plastic or fabric Christmas decorations. They look great tied on presents, and you can put them on your tree when everything's unwrapped.

Here we go!

wrapping up

You can wrap your presents in all sorts of lovely things – cellophane, tissue paper, sparkly fabric, or fur. Then tie ribbon or tinsel round them. Tie on unbreakable Christmas decorations, too!

gift tag

To make a fancy gift tag, cut a butterfly shape from card. Decorate it with tissue paper and glitter glue. Wrap a pipe cleaner round the middle, then tie the gift tag to a parcel.

stick-on pictures

Make your presents extra special by sticking on gorgeous pictures. Try making a Christmas pudding from corrugated card. You can decorate it with card shapes or anything shiny. It looks good enough to eat!

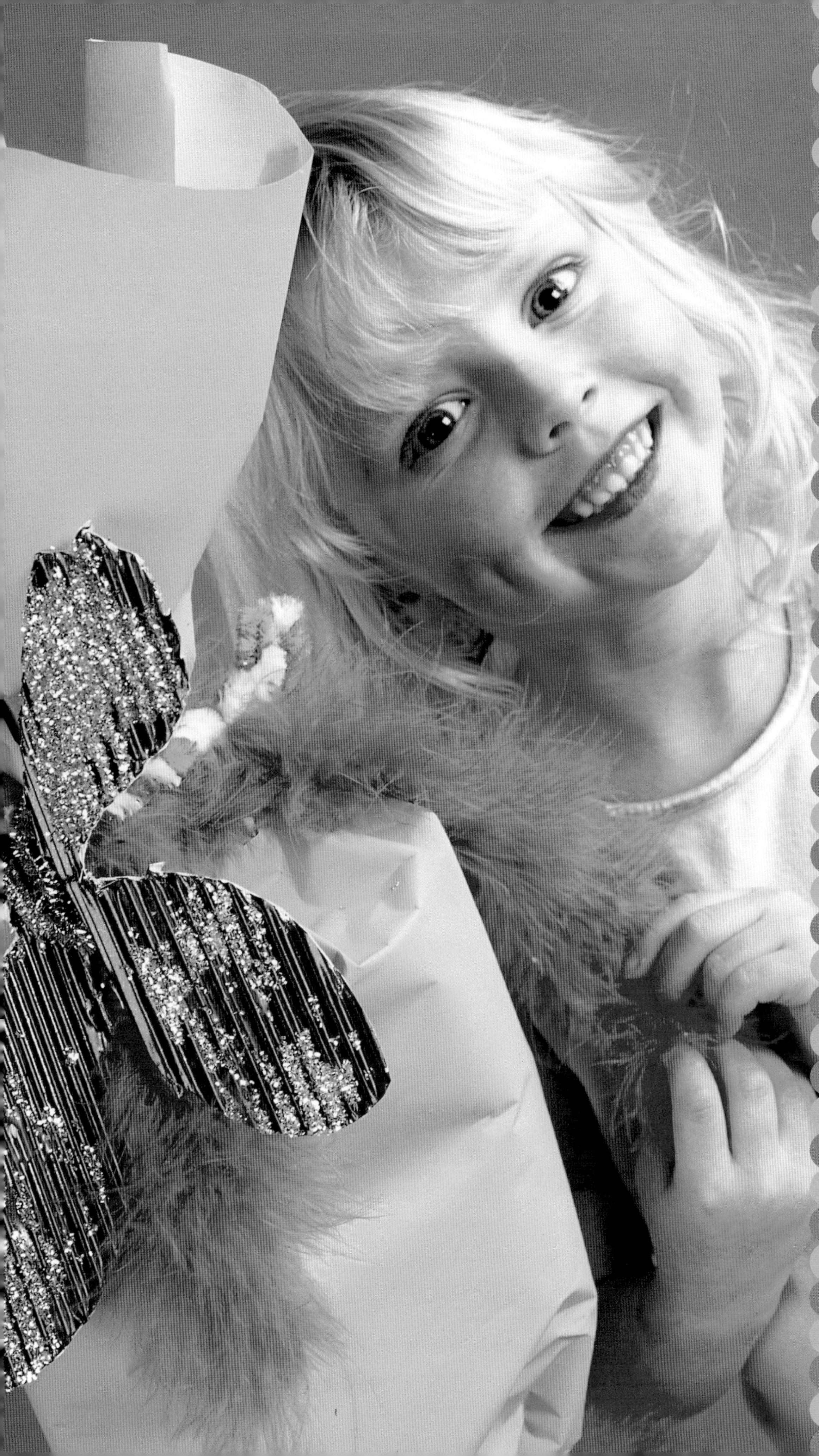

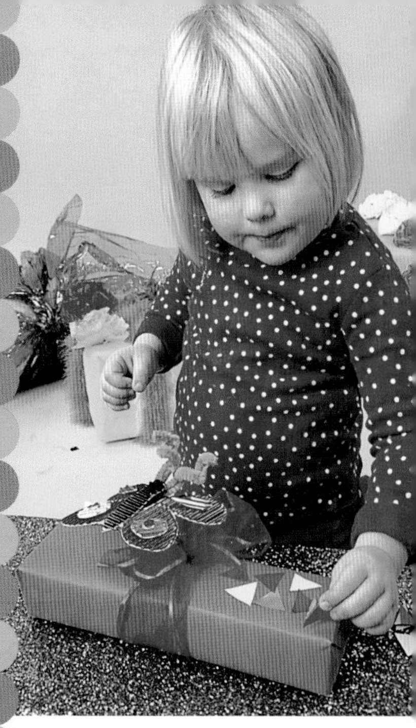

Kid's talk

"I wish it could be Christmas every day."

Emma, age 4 ¼

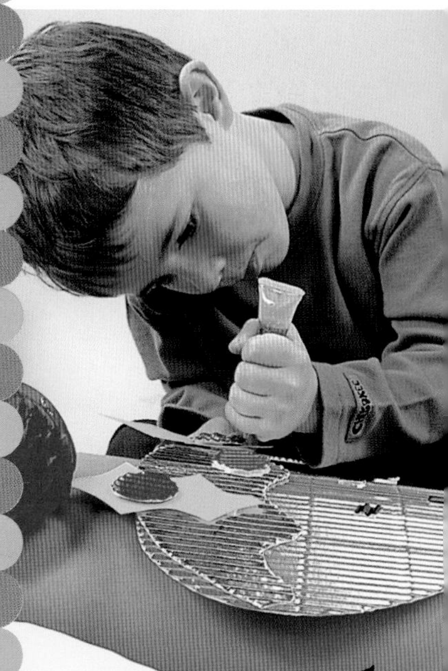

Nellie's knowledge

Christmas is a time for giving, and children love it when you give them your time. What better way to do this than to spend quality time creating Christmas treasures together?

Making decorations,

keeping them safe, and putting them up year after year is a lovely way to bring back happy memories. It also teaches children to respect and look after things.

The joy of giving

is something children can experience when they give a gift they've made themselves. It's a fantastic way for them to share their creativity with you.

Valuable presents

don't have to cost a fortune. I made my mum a vase 25 years ago. She was so delighted when I gave it to her, and it has always been one of her great treasures!

Praise the presents
and Christmas decorations
children make. Telling children
how brilliantly they've
done is so good for all
round confidence.

Boxing Day
is the perfect time
for making things out of
boxes! Empty chocolate
boxes and discarded
packaging are great for
children to recycle and
transform.

Display
your Christmas cards
by pegging them onto lines
of ribbon. Or stick the cards
on boxes, stacked one on top
of another, to make a
Christmas-card tree!

Top up
your art kit
with the ribbons,
wrapping paper, and
shiny bits and bobs left
over from presents
and crackers.

New Year calendars
are really useful. You can
use your recycled bits and
bobs to make a collage, and
buy a little flip calendar
from a stationery shop to
attach to your design.

Have a fun Christmas. Goodbye!